BENEDICITE HUNC CIBUM

Bless This Food

AMAZING GRACES
IN THANKS FOR FOOD

ADRIAN BUTASH

Delacorte Press

Published by
Delacorte Press
Bantam Doubleday Dell Publishing Group, Inc.
1540 Broadway
New York, New York 10036

Library of Congress Cataloging in Publication Data

Bless this food : amazing graces in thanks
for food / [compiled by]
Adrian Butash.
p.   cm.
Includes index.
ISBN 0-385-31106-0
1. Grace at meals.   I. Butash, Adrian.
BL560.B55   1993
291.4'3—dc20   93-12928   CIP

Manufactured in the United States of America

Published simultaneously in Canada

November 1993

10 9 8 7 6 5 4 3 2 1

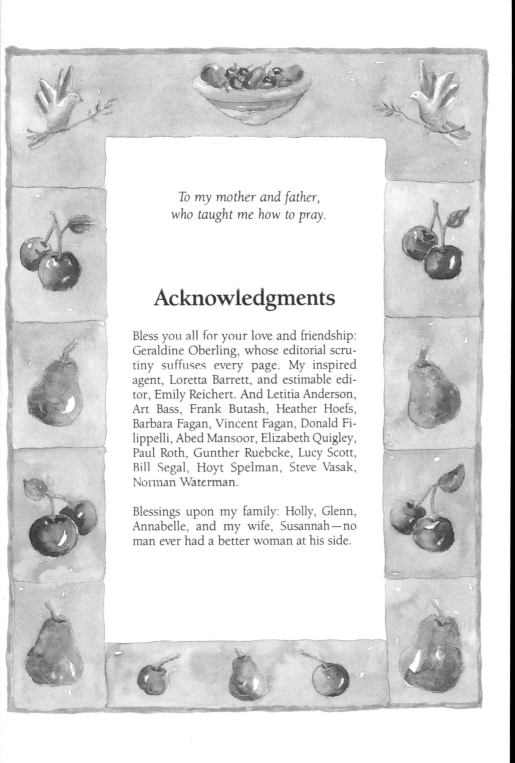

To my mother and father,
who taught me how to pray.

Acknowledgments

Bless you all for your love and friendship: Geraldine Oberling, whose editorial scrutiny suffuses every page. My inspired agent, Loretta Barrett, and estimable editor, Emily Reichert. And Letitia Anderson, Art Bass, Frank Butash, Heather Hoefs, Barbara Fagan, Vincent Fagan, Donald Filippelli, Abed Mansoor, Elizabeth Quigley, Paul Roth, Gunther Ruebcke, Lucy Scott, Bill Segal, Hoyt Spelman, Steve Vasak, Norman Waterman.

Blessings upon my family: Holly, Glenn, Annabelle, and my wife, Susannah—no man ever had a better woman at his side.

Foreword

Open this book to any page, and you will find meaning and beauty in every prayer. Food blessings provide a window through which we can see that we all share a profound spirituality that connects us to humankind, nature, and the infinite.

The thanksgiving food blessing is the prayer said most often in the home. This is its essential beauty. Saying a blessing before a meal can bring us closer to our brothers and sisters, parents, and friends. Asking a friend to choose and recite a food blessing is a wonderful way to welcome that person into a family setting. The occasional gathering for prayer, no matter how brief, can keep the heart and mind in touch with the most fundamental of joys: belonging.

For any child who can read, this book gives young ones an opportunity to lead the family in prayer, to participate actively in a family ritual, rather than remain subordinate, passive members at the table. Children will also discover that food prayers provide an interesting and informative educational experience, stimulating the mind with a variety of subjects: nature, history, spirituality, religion, people, and customs of other cultures throughout the world. Whether impromptu words or a formal prayer, the food blessing is a powerful medium to enrich the meaning of family and bring us into contact with a higher realm of spirituality.

While prayers often derive from specific religious contexts, they may be experienced and enjoyed by all, just as religious music or fine art transcends its origins and has universal appeal. There are many nonreligious prayers that evoke spirituality by virtue of the beauty of the words and the underlying humanity that shines through.

The blessings I have gathered here are a spiritually nourishing basket of poetic fruit—sacred prayers from all times, for all people. Amid these words you will find the soul of humanity, the song of ages. These simple prayers of thanks are a record of mankind's unbroken relationship with God and the divine. The prayers, many of which have been uttered over aeons, have never lost their power.

Contents

Introduction

The sacred texts of the world, such as the Bible, the Koran, the Lotus Sutra, the Hindu Vedic corpus, have a common profound quality. What marks them as sacred is that they are treated as holy documents possessing supreme authority and power, by virtue of their divine origin. Sacred texts are created directly by God or revealed to humankind or recorded by holy prophets. Through the centuries, rebbes, monks and saints have orally passed down such sacred texts as the Pali canon, the sacred Scripture of Theravada Buddhism, and the Torah, which originally was forbidden to be written and was memorized by tannas, who were flawless "repeaters" of the text. Sacred texts are immutable and are considered "closed" texts, which cannot be altered or revised. A distinguishing feature of a sacred text is its beneficence to humanity. While not all food prayers are sacred (including those in this anthology), they all possess some kind of beneficial power for humankind.

For those whose intellectual interest is in what Paul Verlaine called "mere literature," the compelling beauty of these thanksgiving food prayers reveals the noble spirituality of humanity. Prayer is how human beings relate to God, nature, and their place in the divine order of things. Prayer is the principal channel we use in our search for ultimate meaning. Thanksgiving food prayers embody religious and social contexts, encompassing myth, sacred doctrine, rituals, and social and cultural practices.

Sharing food is the most universal cultural experience. Expressing thanks for food was humankind's first act of worship, for food is the gift of life from above. In every culture there are sacred beliefs or divine commandments that require honoring the giver of life — God or the divine principle — through acknowledging the sacred gift of food. By admitting us to his table, God became bound to us in a unique relationship. By admitting God to our table, we experience the love and beauty of that relationship.

The gods command prayers of thanks for food. The Bible has several citations: "And thou shall eat and be satisfied, and bless the Lord your God" (Deut. 8:10). The divine origin of the words of the Koran are better appreciated if you understand that the Koran is to Muslims what Jesus — not the Bible — is to Christianity. A verse from the Koran, the words of Allah, the God of Islam, as recorded under divine guidance by the Prophet Muhammad instructs Muslims on the sacred origins of food and the requirement for food prayers: "Eat of your Lord's provision, and give thanks to Him" (34:15).

While some people may believe that "grace" is a Christian or Western notion, the etymology of the word shows otherwise. The theological notion of *grace* infuses the entire meaning of thankfulness. Grace is the unmerited love of God and the presence of God in us. This presence of divine love is gratuitous. *Gratuitous* (given freely) comes from the Latin *gratuitus* (grateful) and derives from the Latin word for thanks (*gratia*), found in many languages; Old French, *gratus* (thankful); Sanskrit, *grnati* (sing praise). *Grace* in Greek is *charis* (charisma). Charismata is the power of the Holy Spirit. A grace is the thanks-to-God utterance before or after a meal. Food has always been recognized as the unmerited gift from God. Grace is the divine reality underlying all religion and faith — that is, God's loving generosity. In the Hebrew Scriptures it is *hesed* (loving kindness). In the Tao it is found in the love of the Hindu triad Brahma, Vishnu, Siva. In Christian theology, grace is the human transcendent activity of God in every creature.

Whether that expression of thanks (*gratia*) for the gift of spiritual and physical food is voiced in a tribal ritualized saying or uttered silently or sung eloquently, a person's intrinsic spiritual nature imposes a recognition that the very food before him or her is sacred and mysterious and comes to him or her from the beyond.

Consider: The first interhuman act of the newborn child is to experience satisfaction through food. In the first hour of life our senses may transmit ephemeral sight, sound, or touch quanta, but it is the initial ingestion of milk from the mother that constitutes the first interhuman act: nourishment. The immediate response to this nourishment is a systemic and psychic satisfaction, and the hunger-gratification cycle begins at that instant and continues throughout life. The just-born infant's first human experience is a "gift" of milk in response to its sucking instinct and food need, a gratifying experience that has an impact on the infant's psyche on its deepest level. This *gratis experience* is irrevocably imprinted on the newborn's uninscribed mind and is the primordial unconscious analogue to voiced prayer. Our first common human emotional experience is the *gratia response* for food.

The ritualized saying of food prayers in thanks for God's bounty is an acculturated experience derived through social and religious practices. This "imposition" of formal prayer saying is a confirmation of our first primal food experience. It gives form to expressing thankfulness that reaches immediately back to our first minutes of life and is something inherently cognate within us. The *gratia* experience we encounter as infants is transformed and intellectualized over time into an appreciation of food as both spiritual and physical nourishment that is acknowledged in the gratis prayer.

There are four principal types of thanksgiving grace: the silent grace, the spoken grace, the sung grace, the signed grace. I thought it would be nice to include an adult and child's signed grace (prayers 133 and 134). They have a beauty all their own. See for yourself.

While this book is a collection of blessings that civilization has preserved, there are other momentous prayers of thanks that are documented but whose actual words are not known. An intriguing example is two prayers of thanks that, according to the Bible, Jesus offered at the Last Supper. We don't know if the prayers were voiced or silent. Jesus' exact words (if they were spoken) were not recorded by the authors of the New Testament. In the course of the Last Supper, the Bible tells us, "Jesus gave thanks" to God in heaven. The first grace was intoned before Jesus drank the wine, and the second divine *gratia* before he ate the bread. These two thanksgiving prayers of Jesus are sacred mysteries.

The Dead Sea Scrolls document another fascinating prayer of thanks that was a sacred rite of the Essenes, the authors of the scrolls. (*Essene* means "pious one.") This ancient esoteric Jewish sect existed from the second century B.C. to the first century A.D. The scrolls are thus unaffected by either Christian or rabbinical censorship (rabbinic teachers did not permit religious writings to enter Jewish posterity if they did not conform to strict orthodoxy), and they therefore provide an insight into pre–Christian-Jewish ancient literature, customs, and beliefs. One of the key concepts of Jewish eschatology (final days) is the Day of Judgment. A chapter in the scrolls known as "The Messianic Rule" gives a visionary description of the end of the world with the coming of the Messiah and the prescribed conduct for the members of the community in celebrating this miraculous event. At the end of the world there will be a great feast. The Messiah will be at the head of the table, and before him will sit the chiefs of the clans of Israel, the wise men, and all others. The congregation will eat and drink new wine, but not before a prayer of thanks. A priest will bless the first fruits of bread and wine, and then the Messiah will hold his hand over the bread, and each man and woman will be required to recite his or her own blessing. In this remarkably beautiful last rite, the final act of humankind will be to create one's own blessing, to be uttered before the Messiah, "each man in the order of his dignity."

In an ancient Sumerian site called Nippur, a small inscribed tablet that dates from 1700 B.C. was unearthed in 1949. It is known in anthropological circles as the "First Farmers' Almanac" because it offers agricultural advice from a father to his son. Practical instructions are supplemented by the requirement of saying a thanksgiving-for-food prayer, a commandment laid down by Ninurta, son of the "true farmer" Enlil (a principal Sumerian deity). "On the day the seed breaks through the ground . . . say a prayer to Ninkilim."

Historians acknowledge the Sumerians as the very first civilization (3000 B.C.). They lived in Mesopotamia, later known as Babylonia, the cradle of agricultural development. The Sumerian and Near East pantheon had many gods of food, crops and abundance whose thanksgiving prayers did not survive the ages—i.e., Abu, Baal, Dagon, Mot, Nikkal, Ninib, Ninsar, Tammuz. Sumerian mythology and culture were the source of Babylonian, Assyrian, Phoenician, and biblical customs and rituals which evolved into Judaism, Christianity and Islam.

For Muslims, the thanksgiving prayer is the *basmalah* formula *bismi-Llahi-r Rahmani-r-Rahim*, "In the name of God, the Merciful, the Compassionate." *Basmalah* is never omitted before a Muslim meal; it is the equivalent of saying grace. The meal is never ended without uttering the *hamdalah*, the "praise God." The hamdalah (colloq. hamdullah) is the required ending response to the *basmalah*. The Prophet is clear on the motivation for saying grace: "If you are thankful, surely I will increase you" (Koran 14:7).

In the Hindu belief, food cannot be eaten unless it is first offered to God. It then becomes *prasad* (sanctified or observed as holy), something to be eaten that was blessed by God. Hinduism puts great emphasis on the loving reliance upon God. An example of this is seen in prayer 5 from the Bhagavad Gita (Song of the Lord), the most sacred religious text of Hinduism. The Gita is found in the Mahabharata, an extraordinary Sanskrit epic that dates from the second century B.C. Another sublime prayer from antiquity is a paean to Annapurna, a beneficent goddess in India who provides food and bears the fruit of knowledge. She is the corn goddess who nourishes all things as mother (prayer 46).

The Old Testament and New Testament abound with examples of blessings and incorporate into their liturgy food-related ritual, ceremony and metaphor. The New Testament records the sharing of food on numerous occasions. In Luke's Gospel there are thirty-one citations. There are fourteen in John, twenty-six by Mark, and twenty by Matthew. Throughout Corinthians, food and its consumption occupy an important theological position and are mentioned by Paul twenty-two times.

The Last Supper, the final meal eaten by Jesus with his Apostles before the Crucifixion, has been traditionally called the Passover meal. For Christians, the Lord's Prayer (prayer 18), recited at the Lord's Supper, is a universal thanksgiving prayer with its imagery of gratefulness for life-sustaining daily bread. Theologically, the Eucharist is the Christian sacrament commemorating the Last Supper. The word *Eucharist* is derived from the Greek *eucharistia* (thanksgiving). In the celebration of Holy Communion, the consecrated bread and wine are transformed into the body and blood of Jesus Christ. "He that eateth my flesh, and drinketh my blood, dwelleth in me, and I in him" (John 6:56).

Food and associated prayers play a central role in religions of the Far East. Confucianism, founded by Confucius in the sixth century B.C., is one of the two major Chinese ideologies, the other being Taoism (from *Tao* meaning "the Way"). Taoism is based on the annual rotation of the seasons and the harmony and balance of nature. In the *Tasze*, the great sacrifice in the huge Altar Park (the largest altar in the world), offerings of food, rice spirits, and other gifts are placed on the altar and the spirit of heaven is invited by means of a sacred hymn to descend to the altar. Sie-Tsih, the gods of millet and corn, are worshiped in a spring and autumn sacrifice. The modern Chinese expedient *gratia* before the banquet meal, *Duo xie, duo xie* (a thousand thanks, a thousand thanks), is merely the cultural evolution of worship chanted to the many food gods of Chinese antiquity: Chi Ming, Ching Ling Tzu, or Chung Tso. A witty and sophisticated saying in cultural circles that has the elegance of quoting poetry is 人 以 食 为 天 (Ren Yi Shi Wei Tian), "People perceive food to be almost like God."

Shinto is the old native religion of Japan that reveres ancestors and nature spirits. Derived from the Chinese Shen-Tao (way of the gods), Shinto's central belief is *kami*, God, the sacred power that infuses animate and inanimate things. Amaterasu is the most eminent of the Shinto deities. She is the beneficent sun goddess who taught mankind the cultivation of food. Inari is the grain god. *Norito* prayers petition the gods for good harvests. The Setsubun ceremony celebrates the start of a new season of seeds and planting. Its rites involve Neolithic rituals that survive today in technofuturist Japan. A cornucopia of rice, cakes, fish, and vegetables are sacred treasures placed on the altar expressing thanks for the bounty of the earth.

Buddhism's history is rich with reverence for food and thankfulness for its nourishment. The great prince Gautama Sakyamuni experienced full enlightenment while sipping a cup of milk-rice as he meditated the doctrine of nirvana under the Tree of Enlightenment, the Bodhi Tree. Buddhists have used prayers of blessing and offering in everything from the cultivation of crops to the dedication of each plate of food to the betterment of humanity. As exemplified by the Buddhist prayers in this book, food can be truly blessed only when the one giving thanks has lived a life of service to both the universe that has given the food and those who suffer and are without food (prayer 97). Buddhism commands thankfulness for food by its "vow to live a life which is worthy to receive it" (prayer 98).

Native American Indian tribes share a common reverence for the earth and all that is given from its bounty. Animals, harvests and water must be accepted with thankfulness in rituals and prayers. Respect for the food gift is often expressed by asking a plant or animal that must be used for food for its forgiveness in taking its life and explaining why its death was necessary (prayer 89). In Native American thought, human beings are dependent upon the earth, not master over it.

Civilization is synonymous in every sense with the growth of agriculture. Cultivating crops predated the invention of the wheel and writing. The existence in the belief of the power of the first fruits or grains has provided the world with many rituals, beliefs and festivals. The festival calendars of antiquity are based on agriculture. Our modern calendar descends from ancient agricultural calendars.

The cultivation of plants for food, as opposed to the use of plants as they grow naturally in the environment, marked the evolution of humanity from a user of food to a producer of food.

The three main Israelite feasts recorded in the Bible are in part, harvest festivals, in which multitudes of Jews brought fruits and vegetables to the Temple in Jerusalem: Pesach, a feast at the beginning of the barley harvest; Shavuot, a summer feast of the end of the wheat harvest; Sukkot, the autumn ingathering of grapes and cultivated fruits. Of the six major sections of the Mishnah, the first collection of Jewish law (A.D. 200) and one of the earliest surviving works of rabbinic literature, one chapter is devoted to seeds and agriculture, another to festivals. Elal (Hebrew *elul*, "to reap, harvest") is the twelfth month in the Jewish year.

In the Old Testament the breaking of bread symbolized the immutable bond in relationships among all people. The Covenant was reaffirmed through deeply profound meals and feasts. The Hebrew word for *covenant* (*b'rith*) has etymological origins in the Hebrew notion "to eat." The ancient Jewish prayer (6) has been intoned in Jewish homes over the centuries. It is a grace before the meal and is recited before eating the first morsel of bread.

The Jewish liturgy is full of the idea of divine grace interceding to aid humanity. Grace is *Ahabah Rabbah* and thanksgiving *Shemoneh Esreh*. The liturgy requires separate blessings (*b'rachot*) for various categories of food. The blessing over bread (the *hamotzi*) differs from that of cakes and cooked grains; fruits and vegetables have their own blessings, as does wine and fragrances. Inviting poor people to have food with you makes your table an altar and the meal an atonement. Martin Buber helps us realize that our very table is sacred: "One eats in holiness and the table becomes an altar."

There are many ways to analyze and classify food prayers: by country, by culture, by language, by religion, by God, by food, by sacred imagery—to name a few. A definitive analysis of food prayers is beyond the scope of this book. I have divided the prayers here into two broad classifications: food prayers honoring God or gods and food prayers extolling the bounty on earth. All civilizations and all religions through all ages associate food with God or gods; all primitives nonbelievers associate food with a supernatural power or spirits. All recognize the earth's bounty (crops and food) as a reflection of divine goodness.

Food prayers to the gods are created for many reasons: making one's wishes known, honoring the dead in order to show reverence for life, reconciling God(s) with humanity in order to bring good fortune on earth or to assure a place in the afterlife. The recognition of the earth as sacred manifests itself in the ritual and religious life of communities as petitional prayers by the laborers, chants for seed planting and crop proliferation, ceremonials for laying out plots, transmittal of family tradition, and reflection on the concept of home and hearth. Central to all cultures and religions, food is a sacred gift that is the supreme and universal bond of all friendship.

The world's quest for happiness operates within a context of reverence for God through an inimitable link to food. In this uncertain age when ethnic differences divide people, we should strive to embrace our common humanity that is expressed so succinctly in food prayers. These prayers talk to us with the wisdom of the ages and teach us that we are all one family, all one mystical soul. Food prayers throughout history may be seen as evidence of our profound sense of awe in the face of the infinite.

I have chosen to include in this book texts that are not prayers per se, which nevertheless have great spiritual quality, literary merit and an eloquence in expressing mankind's profound debt to God.

ADRIAN BUTASH
Santa Barbara
June 1993

Prayers
to
God in
Heaven

lakshmi demeter prosperina confucius isis mans indra venus buddha yahwe
devi penates tsao wang robigus cwen-sio anat darvi pan fu hsi tammuz

God be in my bread
God be in my head
God be in my body
God be in my arms
God be in me
God be all around me

God be in all things
God be

William C. Segal
Prayer 1

Radiant is the World Soul
Full of splendor and beauty
Full of life
Of Souls Hidden,
Of treasures of the Holy Spirit,
Fountains of strength,
Of greatness and beauty.
Proudly I ascend
Toward the heights of the World Soul
That gives life to the universe.
How majestic the vision
Come, enjoy,
Come, find peace,
Embrace delight,
Taste and see that God is good.
Why spend your substance on what does not
nourish
And your labor on what cannot satisfy?
Listen to me, and you will enjoy what is good,
And find delight in what is truly precious.

Abraham Isaac Kook, 1865–1935

Prayer 2

Praise we the Lord
Of the heavenly kingdom,
God's power and wisdom,
The works of His hand;
As the Father of glory,
Eternal Lord,
Wrought the beginning
Of all His wonders!
Holy Creator!
Warden of men!
First, for a roof,
O'er the children of earth,
He established the heavens,
And founded the world,
And spread the dry land
For the living to dwell in.
Lord Everlasting!
Almighty God!

Caedmon, A.D. *680*
Prayer 3

O Lord of the universe
Please accept all this food
It was given by you
Let it be of service to all
Only you can bless it.

Bhagavad Gita, fifth century B.C.
Prayer 4

The spiritually minded,
who eat in the spirit of service,
are freed from all their sins;
but the selfish,
who prepare food for their own satisfaction,
eat sin.

Living creatures are nourished by food,
and food is nourished by rain;
rain itself is the water of life,
which comes from selfless worship and service.

Bhagavad Gita 3:13–14, fifth century B.C.
Prayer 5

Blessed art thou
O Lord our God
king of the world
who bringest forth bread from the earth.

Traditional Jewish Blessing

Prayer 6

Blessed are You, O Lord our God,
King of the universe
who feeds the whole world with
Your goodness, grace, kindness and mercy.
You give food to all flesh,
for Your kindness is for ever.
Through Your great goodness,
food has never failed us:
may it never fail us,
for the sake of Your great Name,
for You nourish and sustain all beings,
and do good to all,
and provide food for all Your creatures
whom you have created.
Blessed are You, O Lord,
who gives food to all.

The First Blessing, Jewish Grace After Meals

Prayer 7

Thank You, Lord
Wen na régé

Burkina Faso, West Africa
Prayer 8

Lord of Lords, Creator of all things,
  God of all things, God over all gods,
  God of sun and rain,
  You created the earth with a thought
  and us with your breath.

Lord, we brought in the harvest.
  The rain watered the earth,
  the sun drew cassava
  and corn out of the clay. Your mercy
  showered blessing after blessing over our
  country. Creeks grew into rivers; swamps
  became lakes. Healthy fat cows graze on the
  green sea of the savanna. The rain smoothed
  out the clay walls, the mosquitos drowned in
  the high waters.

Lord, the yam is fat like meat,
  the cassava melts on the tongue, oranges
  burst in their peels, dazzling and bright.

Lord, nature gives thanks,
  Your creatures give thanks. Your praise rises in
  us like the great river.

West African Prayer
Prayer 9

In peace let us eat this food which the Lord hath provided for us. Blessed be the Lord in His gifts. Amen.

Glory be to the Father, and to the Son, and to the Holy Ghost, now and always, world without end. Amen.

Armenian Grace
Prayer 10

The Blessing of God
rest upon all those who have been kind to us,
have cared for us, have worked for us,
        have served us,
and have shared our bread with us at this table.

Our merciful God,
reward all of them in your own way.
For yours is the glory and honor forever.
Amen.

St. Cyril of the Coptic Orthodox Church,
Alexandria, A.D. 412
Prayer 11

I thank Thee, O Lord,
    because Thou hast bound me in the bundle of life.
I thank Thee, O Lord,
    because Thou hast saved me from the pit.
I thank Thee, O Lord,
    because Thou hast gladdened me with thy
    Covenant.
I thank Thee, O Lord,
    because Thou hast set thine eye upon me.

The Thanksgiving Hymns, Composed from the Dead Sea Scrolls,
second century B.C.–*first century* A.D.
Prayer 12

The Lord bless you and keep you:
The Lord make His face to shine upon you,
and be gracious unto you:
The Lord lift up His countenance upon you,
and give you peace.

Numbers 6:24–26
Prayer 13

Zeus, beginning of all things,
Of all things the leader,
Zeus, to thee a libation
I pour, of hymns the beginning.

Terpander of Lesbos, c. 676 B.C.
Prayer 14

Creator Spirit, by whose aid
The world's foundations first were laid,
Come, visit every pious mind.
Come, pour thy joy on human kind.

Medieval Latin Hymn, Gregory the Great,
seventh century
Prayer 15

Almighty God, whose loving
hand hath given us all that we possess:
Give us also grace to honor thee with our substance,
remembering the account we must one day give
as faithful stewards of thy bounty;
for the sake of Jesus Christ our Lord.

The Book of Common Prayer, *eighteenth century*
Prayer 16

In a few moments of silence,
let each of us be mindful
of all we have for which to give thanks:
friends, food, hopes, health
and happy memories.

(a moment of silence observed)

So, in giving thanks,
we are blessed.
Amen.

Traditional Christian Blessing
Prayer 17

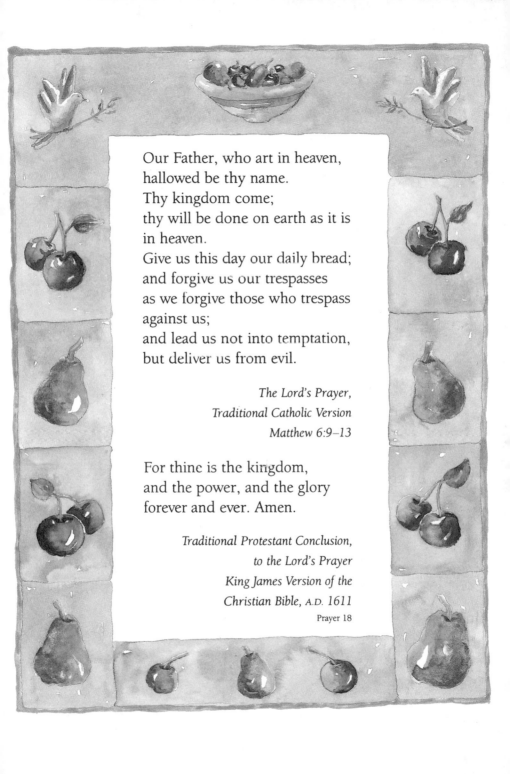

Our Father, who art in heaven,
hallowed be thy name.
Thy kingdom come;
thy will be done on earth as it is
in heaven.
Give us this day our daily bread;
and forgive us our trespasses
as we forgive those who trespass
against us;
and lead us not into temptation,
but deliver us from evil.

The Lord's Prayer,
Traditional Catholic Version
Matthew 6:9–13

For thine is the kingdom,
and the power, and the glory
forever and ever. Amen.

Traditional Protestant Conclusion,
to the Lord's Prayer
King James Version of the
Christian Bible, A.D. 1611

Prayer 18

God who invites us always
   to spiritual delights,
give blessing over your gifts
   so that we might deserve
to partake in the blessed things
   which ought to be added
   to your name.

Let your gifts refresh us,
   Lord,
and let your grace
   comfort us.

Early Christian Grace, sixth century
Prayer 19

Praise God, from whom all blessings flow,
Praise Him, all creatures here below,
Praise Him above, ye heavenly host,
Praise Father, Son, and Holy Ghost. Amen.

Christian Doxology
Prayer 20

O come, let us sing unto the Lord,
Let us joyfully acclaim the Rock of our salvation.
Let us approach Him with thanksgiving,
And acclaim Him with songs of praise.

Jewish Prayer
Prayer 21

Praised be God
Who gave me to eat and to drink.
I shall praise and bless God.

He helps the afflicted.	Praise God.
He clothes the poor.	Praise God.
He is bread for the hungry.	Praise God.
He is a spring for the thirsty.	Praise God.

He gives but none gives to Him.	Praise God.
He lends but none lends to Him.	Praise God.
He increases but none adds to Him.	Praise God.
He teaches but none teaches Him.	Praise God.

There is none save Him.	Praise God.

Liturgy of the Falasha of Abyssinia
Prayer 22

Most worshipful God,
you created humans to walk the earth
with its abundance.
We beg of you, bless our family
with riches and prosperity.
May our farms yield an abundant harvest,
our animals and chickens multiply.
And you our forefathers,
we invite you to look after our well-being.

Ask and demand from us anything,
but protect us from all harm, illness and evil
spirits
which prowl the earth.
We will remember and honor you in the days to
come.
We who partake of this abundant food rejoice
with those who rejoice and live long lives.

This is our heart's desire,
and what our words express.
So let us feast.

Kankana-ey Tribe of the Igorot Indians
Northern Luzon, the Philippines
Prayer 23

Heavenly Father
Bless this food
Make it holy
Let no impurity or greed defile it
The food comes from thee
It is for thy temple
Spiritualize it
We are the petals of thy manifestation
But thou art the flower
Its life, beauty, and loveliness
Permeate our souls with the fragrance of thy presence
Om—peace—amen.

Author Unknown
Prayer 24

Help us, O God, to feed not only
upon bread that nourishes bone and sinew
but upon the radiance of night-blooming cereus,
and the purity of a selfless act, for we are a people
who must feed on bread, beauty, and compassion.

Bless our home, our Father,
that we cherish the bread before there be none,
discover each other for what we are . . .
while we have time.
Amen.

Richard Wong
Prayer 25

In the Name of Allah!
(before eating)
Bi Ismillaahi!

Thanks to Allah, Master of both worlds!
(this and the afterworld)
(after eating)
Al Hamdu Lillaahi Rabbil 'Aalamin!

Traditional Muslim Prayer
Prayer 26

May the blessing of God rest upon you,
May his peace abide with you,
May his presence illuminate your heart
Now and forevermore.

Sufi Blessing
Prayer 27

O Kané! Transform the earth
Let the earth move as in one piece
The land is cracked and fissured

The edible ferns yet grow, O Lono
Let kupukupu cover the dry lands
Gather potatoes as stones on the hills
The rain comes like the side of cliffs
The rain falling from Heaven
The potato falls from the heavens
The wild taro is only taro now
The taro of the mountain patches
The only food that is of the wilds
O Kané
O Kané and Lono! Gods of the husbandmen
Give life to the land

Ancient Hawaiian Harvest Chant
Prayer 28

Salutations!
O Merciful God who provides food for the body
and soul, you have kindly granted what is spread
before us. We thank you.
Bless the loving hands that prepared this meal and
us who are to enjoy it, please.
Homage, homage,
homage to thee!

Tamil Prayer
Prayer 29

O Supreme Lord, the giver of food;
Provide us with healthy and nourishing food.
Grant happiness to all those
That give food in charity
May this food give us health and strength.

Offering this food is the Spirit of God
This food is itself the Spirit of God
It is offered in the Holy Name of God
For the sake of God
Absorbed in this action for the sake of God
May I attain the Supreme Godhead.

I dedicate this food
to the Supreme Godhead Sri Krsna.

Gujarati Mantra
Prayer 30

Wisdom gives life to those who have it.
Happy is the body
that can nourish itself on food of the soul.

When you taste food,
if you know who it is that tastes it,
then you have known Him (Brahman).

Sri Ramana Maharshi
Prayer 31

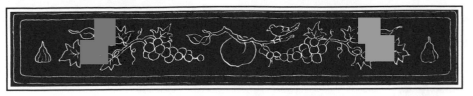

To all else thou hast given us,
O Lord,
we ask for but one thing more:
Give us
grateful hearts.

George Herbert, 1593–1633
Prayer 32

O Lord, that lends me life,
Lend me a heart replete with thankfulness.

William Shakespeare, 1564–1616
Prayer 33

Let us, with a gladsome mind,
Praise the Lord, for He is kind;
For His mercies still endure,
Ever faithful, ever sure.

All things living
He doth feed,
His full hand supplies their need:

Let us with a gladsome mind
Praise the Lord, for He is kind.

John Milton, 1609–1674
Prayer 34

O God Our Father,
the foundation of all goodness,
Who has been gracious to us,
not only in the year that is past
but throughout all the years of our lives;
we give you thanks for your loving kindness
which has filled our days
and brought us to this time and place.

John Wesley, 1703–1791

Prayer 35

Lord of the harvest, hear
    Thy needy servants cry;
Answer our faith's effectual prayer,
    And all our wants supply.

On thee we humbly wait,
    Our wants are in thy view:
The harvest truly, Lord, is great,
    The laborers are few.

Charles Wesley, 1707–1788

Prayer 36

Christ, the gladdener of all, without whom nothing is sweet or pleasant, bless, we beg you, the food and drink of your servants, which you have now provided for our bodily sustenance; and grant that we may use these gifts to praise you, and may enjoy them with grateful hearts; grant too that, just as our body is nurtured by bodily foods, so too our mind may feed on the spiritual nourishment of your Word, through you our Lord.

From the services of Christ's College, Cambridge, England 1535
Prayer 37

O heavenly Father, you have filled the
world with beauty and provided for us in
abundance. Open our eyes to behold your
gracious hand in all your works; that rejoicing
in your whole creation, we may learn to
serve you with gladness.

The Book of Common Prayer, *sixteenth century*
Prayer 38

Offerings are made to thee,
Oxen are slain to thee,
Great festivals are kept for thee,
Pure flames are offered to thee.

Ancient Egyptian Prayer to Hapi,
God of the Nile
Prayer 39

God of my needfulness,
grant me something to eat,
give me milk,
give me sons,
give me herds,
give me meat,
O my Father.

African Morning Invocation
Prayer 40

O God,
I am as one hungry for rice,
parched as one thirsty for tea.
Fill my so empty heart.
Amen.

China

Prayer 41

God,
we thank you for all your gifts.
This day, this night,
These fruits, these flowers,
these trees, these waters—
With all these treasures
you have endowed us.
The heat of the sun,
the light of the moon,
the songs of the birds
and the coolness of the breeze,
The green, green grass
like a mattress of velvet.
All owe their existence to your grace.
Dear God, may we forever breathe
the breath of your love
And every moment be aware
of your presence above.

Pakistan

Prayer 42

Lord Christ, we pray thy mercy on our table spread,
And what thy gentle hands have given thy men
Let it by thee be blessed: whate'er we have
Came from thy lavish heart and gentle hand,
And all that's good is thine, for thou art good.
And ye that eat, give thanks for it to Christ,
And let the words ye utter be only peace,
For Christ loved peace: it was himself that said,
Peace I give unto you, my peace I leave with you.
Grant that our own may be a generous hand
Breaking the bread for all poor men, sharing the food.
Christ shall receive the bread thou gavest his poor,
And shall not tarry to give thee reward.

Alcuin of York, 735–804
Prayer 43

Praised are You, Lord our
God, King
of the universe, for all the
nourishment
and produce of the field, for the lovely
and spacious land which You
gave to our fathers as a
heritage to eat of its fruit and
enjoy its good gifts. Have
mercy, Lord our God, on Your
people Israel, on Your altar
and Your shrine. Speedily
rebuild the holy city of
Jerusalem. Bring us there and
gladden us with the
restoration of our land. May
we eat of its fruit and enjoy
its good gifts. May we bless
You for it in holiness and
purity.

Jewish Blessing
Prayer 44

Ishvari, who ever giveth food,
Bestower of happiness to all,
who advanceth all people,
Presiding Devi over the city of Kashi,
Vessel of mercy, grant me aid.

From the Mahabharata, 200 B.C.–A.D. *200*
Prayer 45

O Devi, clad in fine garment
Ever giver of rice, Sinless One,
Who delights in the dance of Shiva.
O Annapurna! Obeisance to thee.

Hymns to the Goddess, c. 200 B.C.
Prayer 46

Let me meditate on the glorious
Supreme Being—the Sun—which brightens all the
three worlds—the Heaven, the Earth, and the
Nether land. May He enlighten our hearts and direct
our understanding.

The Gayatri Hymn, India, c. 1500 B.C.
Prayer 47

For the Lord your God
is bringing you
into a good land,

a land
of flowing streams,
with springs and underground waters
welling up in valleys and hills,
a land of wheat and barley,
of vines and fig trees and pomegranates,
a land of olive trees and honey,
a land where you may eat bread without
                    scarcity,
where you will lack nothing,
a land whose stones are iron
and from whose hills you may mine copper.

You shall eat your fill
and bless the Lord your God
for the good land
he has given you.

Deuteronomy 8:7–11
Prayer 48

Author of my well-being,
source of knowledge,
fount of holiness, height of glory,
all-mightiness of eternal splendor!

I shall choose that which
He shall have taught me
and I shall rejoice in that which
He shall have appointed unto me.

When I put forth my hands and my feet,
I shall bless His Name;
when I go out or when I go in,
when I sit down or when I rise up,
and upon my bed shall I sing unto Him.
I shall bless Him with the offering
which comes forth from my lips
for the sake of all which He has established
unto men,
and before I lift up my hands to partake
of the delicious fruits of the earth.

Dead Sea Scrolls, second century B.C.*–first century* A.D.
Prayer 49

Cast thy bread upon the waters: for thou
shalt find it after many days.

Ecclesiastes 11:1
Prayer 50

Blessed are you, Lord.
You have fed us from our earliest days;
you give food to every living creature.
Fill our hearts with joy and delight.
Let us always have enough
and something to spare for works of mercy
in honor of Christ Jesus, our Lord.
Through him may glory, honor
    and power be yours forever.

Fourth-century Prayer, Author Unknown
Prayer 51

We thank you, Father,
for the life and knowledge you
    have revealed to us
through your child Jesus
Glory be yours through all ages.
As grain once scattered on the
    hillside
was in this broken bread made
    one,
so from all lands may we be
    gathered
into your kingdom by your Son.

The Didache, c. A.D. 150
Prayer 52

For the fruits of this creation,
  Thanks be to God.
For the gifts to every nation,
  Thanks be to God.
For the plowing, sowing, reaping,
Silent growth while we are sleeping,
Future needs in earth's safe-keeping,
  Thanks be to God.

In the just reward of labor,
  God's will be done.
In the help we give our neighbor,
  God's will be done.
In the world-wide task of caring,
For the hungry and despairing,
In the harvest we are sharing,
  God's will be done.

Fred Pratt Green, 1903
Prayer 53

As thou hast set the moon in the sky
to be the poor man's lantern,
so let thy Light shine in my dark life
and lighten my path;
as the rice is sown in the water
and brings forth grain in great abundance,
so let thy word be sown in our midst
that the harvest may be great;
and as the banyan sends forth its branches
to take root in the soil,
so let thy Life take root in our lives.

Author Unknown
Prayer 54

O Thou, who kindly doth provide
For ev'ry creature's want!
We bless the God of Nature wide
For all Thy goodness lent.
And if it please Thee, heavenly Guide,
May never worse be sent;
But, whether granted or denied,
Lord, bless us with content.

Robert Burns, 1759–1796
Prayer 55

Sweet is the work, my God, my King,
to praise thy name, give thanks and sing.

Fasola Folk of the Rural South, United States
Prayer 56

May the abundance of this table never fail
and never be less, thanks to the blessings of
God, who has fed us and satisfied our needs.
To him be the glory for ever. Amen.

Armenian Grace from Lebanon
Prayer 57

Jesus took the loaves,
and when he had given thanks,
he distributed to those who were
seated,
so also the fish,
as much as they wanted.

John 6:11
Prayer 58

Whether therefore ye eat,
    or drink, or whatsoever ye do,
Do all to the glory of God.

1 Corinthians 10:31
Prayer 59

One does not live by bread alone,
but by every word that comes
from the mouth of God.

Matthew 4:4
Prayer 60

O God, our Father, be Thou the Unseen
Guest at our table, and fill our
Hearts with Thy Love.

Author Unknown

Prayer 61

Lord, you clothe the lilies,
you feed the birds of the sky,
you lead the lambs to pasture,
and the deer to the waterside,
you multiplied loaves and fishes,
and changed the water to wine;
come to our table as giver,
and as our guest to dine.

Mealtime Blessing

Prayer 62

Bless, O Lord, the plants,
the vegetation,
and the herbs of the field,
that they may grow
and increase to fullness
and bear much fruit.
And may the fruit of the land
remind us of the spiritual fruit
we should bear.

Coptic Orthodox Liturgy, Egypt

Prayer 63

I am food, I am food, I am food.

I am the food-eater, I am the food-eater, I am the food-eater.

I am the combining agent, I am the combining agent, I am the combining agent.

I am the first-born of the world-order, earlier than the gods, in the center of immortality.

Whoso gives me, he surely does save thus.

I, who am food, eat the eater of food. I have overcome the world. I am brilliant like the sun.

Mystical Chant from the Upanishad, *c. 900* B.C.
Prayer 64

We entreat thee, O Lord, mercifully to bless
the air and the dews, the rains and the winds;
that through thy heavenly benediction all
may be saved from dearth and famine, and
enjoy the fruits of the earth in abundance and
plenty; for the eyes of all wait upon thee, O Lord,
who givest them their meat in due season.

The Eucharist in India
Prayer 65

I shall sing a song of praise to God:
    Strike the chords upon the drum.

God who gives us all good things—
    Strike the chords upon the drum—

Wives, and wealth, and wisdom.
    Strike the chords upon the drum.

Balubas of Zaire
Prayer 66

O God, you have formed heaven and earth;
You have given me all the goods
that the earth bears!
Here is your part, my God.
Take it!

Pygmies of Zaire
Prayer 67

A circle of friends is a blessed thing.
Sweet is the breaking of bread
   with friends.
For the honor of their presence
at our board
We are deeply grateful, Lord.

Thanks be to Thee for friendship shared,
Thanks be to Thee for food prepared.
Blessed Thou the cup; bless Thou
the bread;
Thy blessing rest upon each head.

Walter Rauschenbusch, 1861–1918
Prayer 68

Enter, O Lord, enter this home
and bless each of us one by one
and also bless our loved ones.
Grant that we enjoy the fruits of
your redemptive peace.
With a blessed glance
deliver anything that might harm us.
Shower your divine grace
over each of us that we might
share this bread without sorrow.
With your power, Lord, free us
from anything that might hurt
us in mind, soul and body. Amen.

Sister Judith Marie Saenz
Prayer 69

Come, you thankful people,
  Come, raise the song of harvest home:
All is safely gathered in,
  Ere the winter storm begin;
God, our Maker, does provide for our wants
  to be supplied;
Come to God's own temple, come, raise the
  song of harvest home.

All the world is God's own field,
  Fruit unto his praise to yield;
Wheat and tares together sown,
  Unto joy or sorrow grown.
First the blade, and then the ear,
  Then the full corn shall appear;
Grant, O harvest Lord, that we
  wholesome grain and pure may be.

Henry Alford, 1810–1871
Prayer 70

*Prayers
in Thanks
for the
Bounty
of the
Earth*

Earth, when I am about to die
I lean upon you.
Earth, while I am alive
I depend upon you.

Ashanti, Central Ghana tribe
Prayer 71

Here with flowers I interweave my friends.
Let us rejoice!
Our common house is the earth.

I am come too,
here I am standing;
now I am going to forge songs,
make a stem flowering with songs,
oh my friend!
God has sent me as a messenger.
I am transformed into a poem.

Pre-Hispanic Nahuatl Blessing, thirteenth century B.C.
Prayer 72

And now, O friends,
hear the dream of a word:
Each spring gives us life,
the golden ear of corn refreshes us,
the tender ear of corn becomes a necklace for us.
We know that the hearts of our friends are true.

Nahuatl Prayer (Mexico), sixteenth century
Prayer 73

Recall the face of the poorest and
most helpless man whom you
may have seen and ask yourself
if the step you contemplate is
going to be of any use to him.
Will it restore him to a control
over his own life and destiny?
Will it lead to self rule for the hungry
and spiritually starved millions of
our fellow men?

If so, then you will
find your doubts and yourself
melting away.

Mohandas Gandhi, 1869–1948
Prayer 74

Let us live together, eat together
together, let us do noble deeds and share the fruits
Let us understand each other, casting aside
    jealousy and ill-will
Let us all work for peace and peace alone.

Hindu Prayer
Prayer 75

Mother Earth, you who give us food,
whose children we are and on whom we depend,
please make this produce you give us flourish
and make our children and animals grow. . . .

Children, the earth is the mother of man,
because she gives him food. . . .

Rigoberta Menchú, Nobel Peace Prize 1992
Prayer 76

Make us worthy, Lord,
To serve our fellow-men
Throughout the world who live and die
In poverty or hunger.

Give them, through our hands
This day their daily bread,
And by our understanding love,
Give peace and joy.

Mother Teresa of Calcutta Nobel Peace Prize 1979
Prayer 77

All life is your own,
All fruits of the earth
Are fruits of your womb,
Your union, your dance.
Lady and Lord,
We thank you for blessings and abundance.
Join with us, Feast with us, Enjoy with us!
Blessed be.

Starhawk
Prayer 78

These offers are not piled high,
They are not heaped high.
It is only a small bit,
It is only a humble amount.
But grant me your divine pardon,
Grant us your divine forgiveness.
Receive this humble branch of pine,
Receive this humble bit of incense,
Receive this humble cloud of smoke.
Receive then; your holy sun has gone over the hill,
Your holy year has passed.
Take this for the holy end of the year,
Take this for the holy end of the day.

Zinacanteán Indians, Mexico
Prayer 79

Thank you, heavenly Father,
for my bread,
my dad and mother and my bed. Amen.

Child's Prayer of Thanks
Prayer 80

The smel of new breade is comfortable to the heade
and to the herte.

Author Unknown, c. 1400
Prayer 81

Heap high the farmer's wintry hoard!
Heap high the golden corn!

No richer gift has autumn poured
From out her lavish horn!

So let the good old crop adorn
The hills our fathers trod;

Still let us, for His golden corn,
Send up our thanks to God!

John Greenleaf Whittier, 1807–1892
Prayer 82

We return thanks to our mother,
  the earth, which sustains us.
We return thanks to the rivers and streams,
  which supply us with water.
We return thanks to all herbs,
  which furnish medicines for the cure of our diseases.
We return thanks to the corn, and to her sisters,
  the beans and squashes,
  which give us life.
We return thanks to the bushes and trees,
  which provide us with fruit.
We return thanks to the wind,
  which, moving in the air, has banished diseases.
We return thanks to the moon and stars,
  which have given to us their light
  when the sun was gone.
We return thanks to our grandfather Hé-no,
  that he has protected his grandchildren
  from witches and reptiles,
  and has given to us his rain.
We return thanks to the sun,
  that he has looked upon the earth
  with a beneficent eye.
Lastly, we return thanks to the Great Spirit,
  in whom is embodied all goodness,
  and who directs all things
  for the good of his children.

Iroquois Indians
Prayer 83

O God, give me light in my heart
and light in my tongue
and light in my hearing
and light in my sight
and light in my feeling
and light in all my body
and light before me
and light behind me.

Give me, I pray Thee,
light on my right hand
and light on my left hand
and light above me
and light beneath me,
O Lord, increase light within me
and give me light
and illuminate me.

Ascribed to Muhammad, c. A.D. 570–632
Prayer 84

From the sky you send rain on the hills,
and the earth is filled with your blessings.
You make the grass grow for the cattle
and plants for man to use
so that he can grow his crops
and produce wine to make him happy,
olive oil to make him cheerful,
and bread to give him strength.

Psalm 104:13–15
Prayer 85

Let the people praise thee, O God:
    let all people praise thee.
Then shall the earth bring forth her increase:
    and God, even our own God,
        shall give us his blessing.
God shall bless us:
    and all the ends of the world
    shall fear him.

Psalm 67
Prayer 86

Deep peace
  of the running wave to you,
Deep peace
  of the quiet earth to you,
Deep peace
  of the flowing air to you,
Deep peace
  of the shining star to you.

Gaelic Blessing
Prayer 87

For the hay and the corn
  and the wheat that is reaped,
For the labor well done,
  and the barns that are heaped,
For the sun and the dew
  and the sweet honeycomb,
For the rose and the song,
  and the harvest brought home—
Thanksgiving! Thanksgiving!

Traditional Hymn, England
Prayer 88

I am sorry I had to kill thee, Little Brother,
But I had need of thy meat.
My children were hungry and crying for food.
Forgive me, Little Brother.
I will do honor to thy courage, thy strength,
   and thy beauty.
See, I will hang thine horns on this tree.
I will decorate them with red streamers.
Each time I pass, I will remember thee and
   do honor to thy spirit.
I am sorry I had to kill thee.
Forgive me, Little Brother.
See, I smoke to thy memory,
I burn tobacco.

American Indians
Prayer 89

Footprints I make! I go to the field with eager haste.
Footprints I make! Amid rustling leaves I stand.
Footprints I make! Amid yellow blossoms I stand.
Footprints I make! I stand with exultant pride.
Footprints I make! I hasten homeward with a burden of
   gladness.
Footprints I make! There's joy and gladness in my home.
Footprints I make! I stand amidst a day of contentment!

Osage Indians
Prayer 90

I am the one whose praise echoes on high.
I adorn all the earth.
I am the breeze that nurtures all things green.
I encourage blossoms to flourish with ripening fruits.
I am led by the spirit to feed the purest streams.
I am the rain coming from the dew
that causes the grasses to laugh with the joy of life.
I am the yearning for good.

Hildegard of Bingen, 1098–1179
Prayer 91

O Great Spirit, Creator and source of every
blessing, we pray that you will bring peace to all
our brothers and sisters of this world. Give us
wisdom to teach our children to love, to respect
and to be kind to each other. Help us to learn to
share all the good things that you provide for us.
Bless all who share this meal with us today. We ask
your special blessing on those who are hungry
today, especially little children. Help us to be just
and to bring your peace to all the earth. Praise
and Thanksgiving be to you, Amen.

Author Unknown
Prayer 92

As for the leaves, that in the garden bloom,
my love for them is great, as is the good dealt
by the eternal hand, that tends them all.

Dante Alighieri, 1265–1321
La Divina Commedia, *Canto XXVI*
Prayer 93

Bless our hearts
to hear in the
breaking of bread
the song of the universe.

Father John Giuliani
Prayer 94

Be present at our table, Lord,
Be here and everywhere adored
Thy creatures bless, and grant that we
May feast in Paradise with Thee.

John Wesley, 1703–1791
Prayer 95

The beauty of the trees,
the softness of the air,
the fragrance of the grass,
      speaks to me.

The summit of the mountain,
the thunder of the sky,
the rhythm of the sea,
      speaks to me.

The faintness of the stars,
the freshness of the morning,
the dewdrop on the flower,
      speaks to me.

The strength of the fire,
the taste of salmon,
the trail of the sun,
and the life that never goes away,
      they speak to me.

And my heart soars.

Chief Dan George
Prayer 96

If beings knew, as I know, the result of giving and
sharing, they would not eat without having given,
nor would they allow the stain of meanness to obsess
them and take root in their minds. Even if it were
their last morsel, their last mouthful, they would not
enjoy eating without having shared it, if there were
someone to share it with.

Teachings of the Buddha, fifth century B.C.
Prayer 97

This food comes from the Earth and the Sky,
It is the gift of the entire universe
And the fruit of much hard work;
I vow to live a life which is worthy to receive it.

Grace of the Bodhisattva Buddhists
Prayer 98

The garden is rich with diversity
With plants of a hundred families
In the space between the trees
With all the colors and fragrances
Basil, mint and lavender,
God keep my remembrance pure,
Raspberry, Apple, Rose,
God fill my heart with love,
Dill, anise, tansy,
Holy winds blow in me.
Rhododendron, zinnia,
May my prayer be beautiful
May my remembrance O God
   be as incense to thee
In the sacred grove of eternity
As I smell and remember
The ancient forests of earth.

Chinook Psalter
Prayer 99

The bread is not our food.
What feeds us in the bread is God's eternal Word,
is spirit and is life.

Angelus Silesius, 1624–1677
Prayer 100

First, let us reflect on our own work
  and the effort of those who brought us this food.
Secondly, let us be aware of the quality of our deeds
  as we receive this meal.
Thirdly, what is most essential
  is the practice of mindfulness
  which helps us transcend greed, anger, and delusion.
Fourthly, we appreciate this food
  which sustains the good health of our body and mind.
Fifthly, in order to continue our practice for all beings
  we accept this offering.

Zen Buddhist Prayer
Prayer 101

O thou cereal deity, we worship thee.
Thou hast grown very well this year,
and thy flavor will be sweet. Thou art
good. The goddess of fire will be glad, and
we also shall rejoice greatly. O thou god,
O thou divine cereal, do thou nourish the
people. I now partake of thee. I worship
thee and give thee thanks.

Ainos, Japan
Prayer 102

I enter into the House of the Red Rock
Made holy by visiting gods,
And into the House of Blue Water
I am come.
Enter me, Spirit of my forgotten Grandmother,
That curtains of rain may hang
All dark before me,
That tall corn may shake itself
Above my head.

Navajo and Blackfoot Indians
Prayer 103

I inform thee that I intend to eat thee.
Mayest thou always keep me to ascend,
So that I may always be able to reach
the tops of mountains,
and may I never be clumsy!
I ask this from thee, Sunflower-Root.
Thou art the greatest of all in mystery.

Thompson Indians of British Columbia
Prayer 104

May this Sabbath
lift our spirits,
lighten our hearts.

At Candlelighting

Let us bless the source of life
that ripens fruit on the vine
as we hallow the Sabbath day
in remembrance of creation.

Sanctification over Wine

Washing the hands, we call to mind
the holiness of the body.

Washing the Hands

Let us bless the source of life
that brings forth bread from the earth.

Blessing over Bread

Let us acknowledge the source of life
for the earth and for nourishment.
May we protect the earth
that it may sustain us,
and let us seek sustenance
for all who inhabit the world.

Blessing After the Meal

Marcia Falk
Prayer 105

Greeting, Father's Clansman,
I have just made a robe for you, this is it.
Give me a good way of living.
May I and my people safely reach the next year.
May my children increase; when my sons go to war,
may they bring horses.
When my son goes to war, may he return with
black face.
When I move, may the wind come to my face,
may the buffalo gather toward me.

This summer may the plants thrive,
may the cherries be plentiful.
May the winter be good, may illness not reach me.
May I see the new grass of summer,
may I see the full-sized leaves when they come.
May I see the spring.
May I with all my people safely reach it.

Crow Indians
Prayer 106

Prayer, the Church's banquet, Angels' age,
  God's breath in man returning to his birth,
The soul in paraphrase, heart in pilgrimage,
  The Christian plummet, sounding heaven and
  earth;
Engine against the Almighty, sinner's tower,
  Reversed thunder, Christ-side-piercing spear,
The six-days' world transposing in an hour,
  A kind of tune, which all things hear and
  fear;
Softness, and peace, and joy, and love,
  and bliss,
  Exalted manna, gladness of the best,
  Heaven in ordinary, man well drest,
The milky way, the bird of Paradise,
  Church-bells beyond the stars heard,
  The soul's blood,
  The land of spices; something understood.

George Herbert, 1593–1633
Prayer 107

For the order and constancy of nature; for the
beauty and bounty of the world; for day and
night, summer and winter, seed-time and harvest;
for the varied gifts of loveliness and use which
every season brings:
  We praise thee.

John Hunter
Prayer 108

Pity me, pity me!
Father, pity me!

Pity me, pity me!
Father, pity me!

I cry for thirst:
see, I am crying!
I cry for thirst:
see, I am crying!

I have naught to eat,
I've nothing;
I have naught to eat,
I've nothing.

Arapaho Indian Chant
Prayer 109

The lands around my dwelling
Are more beautiful
From the day
When it is given me to see
Faces I have never seen before.
All is more beautiful,
All is more beautiful,
And life is thankfulness.
These guests of mine
Make my house grand.

Eskimo
Prayer 110

Mmmm . . . *hmmm*, mymymy . . . and then I went on,
and God blessed me with my home, and I thank
him for that . . . It may not be what you think it
should be . . . but I thank God that he gave it to me . . .
I got a roof over my head, thank you, Lord . . . I'm
not *braggin'*, children, just thankin' God . . .

Marion Williams, American Gospel Singer
Prayer 111

He gives them shelter from life's stormy weather.
Gives them love to keep them together;
When life gets like a ship on a raging sea
And when the stage of life grows cold,
Somebody helps us play our role . . .
If God is dead, who's that living in my soul?

If my soul had windows, I'd leave them open so
    the world could see
The ugly scars upon those hands that bled for
    you and me.
There's a bridge you can cross if you will
The toll was paid on Golgotha's hill.
If God is dead, who's that living in my soul?

Lawrence Reynolds, 1969
Prayer 112

So high we wave our hands to the ricelands,
To hail the grain blown to distant lands.
O come spirits of the ricefield,
From where you've wandered
Come back we plead.

Igorot Indians, the Philippines
Prayer 113

Nicely, nicely, nicely, away in the East,
the rain clouds care for little corn plants
as a mother cares for her baby.

Zuni Corn Ceremony
Prayer 114

Rev'rent our hearts turn unto the
One who brings to us
Long life and children, peace,
And the gifts of strength and food.
Rev'rent our hearts turn unto our Mother Corn!

Rev'rent our hearts turn unto the
Source whence come to us
Long life and children, peace,
And the gifts of strength and food,
Gifts from Tira'wa, sent through our Mother Corn.

Pawnee Indians
Prayer 115

This ritual is one
This food is one
We who offer the food are one
The fire of hunger is also one
All action is one
We who understand this are one.

An Ancient Hindu Blessing
Before Meals
Prayer 116

The cow from whom all plenty flows,
Obedient to her saintly lord,
Viands to suit each taste outpoured.
Honey she gave, and roasted grain,
Mead sweet with flowers, and sugar-cane.
Each beverage of Flavor rare,
And food of every sort, were there:
Hills of hot rice, and sweetened cakes,
And curdled milk, and soup in lakes.
Vast beakers flowing to the brim
With sugared drink prepared for him;
And dainty sweetmeats, deftly made,
Before the hermit's guests were laid.

Hindu Poem
Prayer 117

Wheresoe'er I turn mine eyes
Around on earth or toward the skies,
I see Thee in the starry field,
I see Thee in the harvest's yield,
In every breath, in every sound,
An echo of thy name is found.
The blade of grass, the simple flower,
Bear witness to Thy matchless pow'r.
My every thought, Eternal God of Heaven,
Ascends to Thee, to whom all praise be given.

Abraham ibn Ezra, 1092–1167
Prayer 118

Eternal Spirit of Justice and Love,
At this time of Thanksgiving we would be aware
   of our dependence on the earth and on the
   sustaining presence of other human beings
   both living and gone before us.
As we partake of bread and wine, may we
   remember that there are many for whom
   sufficient bread is a luxury, or for whom
   wine, when attainable, is only an escape.
Let our thanksgiving for Life's bounty include a
   commitment to changing the world, that
   those who are now hungry may be filled and
   those without hope may be given courage.
Amen.

Congregation of Abraxas
Prayer 119

I'm an Indian.
I think about common things like this pot.
The bubbling water comes from the rain cloud.
It represents the sky.
The fire comes from the sun
which warms us all, men, animals, trees.
The meat stands for the four-legged creatures,
our animal brothers,
who gave of themselves so that we should live.
The steam is living breath.
It was water, now it goes up to the sky,
becomes a cloud again.
These things are sacred.
Looking at that pot full of good soup,
I am thinking how, in this simple manner,
The great Spirit takes care of me.

John Lame Deer, Sioux Indian
Prayer 120

He left it for us.
Something that should be for the people's happiness
They will be strong in body from it.
He left us all this food.
He scattered this all over the Earth.
Now we will give *one* thanks.
That he has left us all this food to live on.
On this Earth.
This is the way it should be in our minds.

Seneca Indians
Prayer 121

So often bread is taken for granted,
Yet there is so much of beauty in bread—
Beauty of the sun and the soil,
Beauty of human toil.
Winds and rains have caressed it,
Christ, Himself, blessed it.

Christian Prayer
Prayer 122

When we eat the good bread, we are
eating months of sunlight, weeks of rain
and snow from the sky, richness out of
the earth. We should be great, each of us
radiant, full of music and full of stories.
Able to run the way clouds do, able to
dance like the snow and the rain. But
nobody takes time to think that he eats all
these things and that sun, rain, snow are
all a part of himself.

Monica Shannon
Prayer 123

When you arise in the morning,
give thanks for the morning light,
for your life and strength.
Give thanks for your food
and the joy of living.

If you see no reason for giving thanks,
the fault lies in yourself.

Tecumseh, Chief of the Shawnee Indians,
1768–1813
Prayer 124

The sacred blue corn seed I am planting,
In one night it will grow and flourish,
In one night the corn increases,
In the garden of the House God.

The sacred white corn seed I am planting
In one day it will grow and ripen
In one day the corn increases
In its beauty it increases.

Navajo Indians
Prayer 125

Be a gardener,
dig a ditch,
toil and sweat,
and turn the earth upside down
and seek the deepness
and water the plants in time.
Continue this labor
and make sweet floods to run
and noble and abundant fruits
to spring.
Take this food and drink
and carry it to God
as your true worship.

Julian of Norwich, c. 1373
Prayer 126

So once a year we throng
Upon a day apart,
To praise the Lord with feast and song,
In thankfulness of heart.

Arthur Guiterman, 1871–1943
Prayer 127

Thank God for home,
And crisp, fair weather,
And loving hearts
That meet together—
And red, ripe fruit
And golden grain—
And dear Thanksgiving
Come again!

Nancy Byrd Turner
Prayer 128

All that I have comes from my Mother!
I give myself over to this pot.
My thoughts are on the good,
the healing properties of this food.
My hands are balanced, I season well!

I give myself over to this pot.
Life is being given to me.
I commit to sharing, I feed others.
I feed She Who Feeds Me.

I give myself over to this gift.
I adorn this table with food.
I invite lovers and friends to come share.
I thank you for this gift.
All that I have comes from my Mother!

Luisah Tesh
Prayer 129

We thank thee Lord
for happy hearts
For rain and sunny weather.
We thank thee Lord
for this our food
And that we are together.

Helen Armstrong Straub
Prayer 130

We eat and we are revived, and we give thanks
to the lives that were ended to nourish our own.
May we merit their sacrifice, and honor
their sparks of holiness
through our deeds of loving kindness.

We give thanks to the Power that makes for Meeting,
for our table has been a place of dialogue and friendship.

We give thanks to Life.
May we never lose touch with the simple joy and wonder
of sharing a meal.

Rabbi Rami M. Shapiro
Prayer 131

All is beautiful,
All is beautiful,
All is beautiful, indeed.

Now the Mother Earth
And the Father Sky,
    Meeting, joining one another,
    Helpmates ever, they.
    All is beautiful,
    All is beautiful,
    All is beautiful, indeed . . .

And the white corn
And the yellow corn,
    Meeting, joining one another,
    Helpmates ever, they.
    All is beautiful,
    All is beautiful,
    All is beautiful, indeed . . .

Life-that-never-passeth,
Happiness-of-all-things,
    Meeting, joining one another,
    Helpmates ever, they.
    All is beautiful,
    All is beautiful,
    All is beautiful, indeed.

Now all is beautiful,
All is beautiful,
All is beautiful, indeed.

Navaho Indians
Prayer 132

Grace in American Sign Language

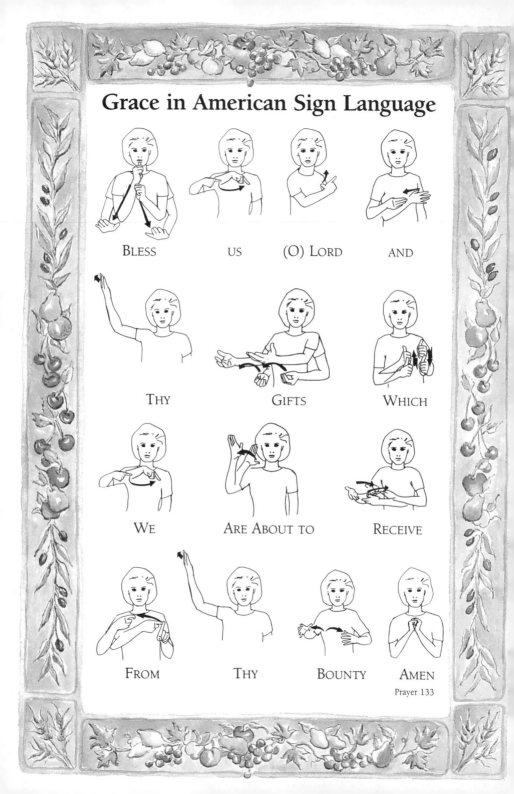

BLESS US (O) LORD AND

THY GIFTS WHICH

WE ARE ABOUT TO RECEIVE

FROM THY BOUNTY AMEN

Prayer 133

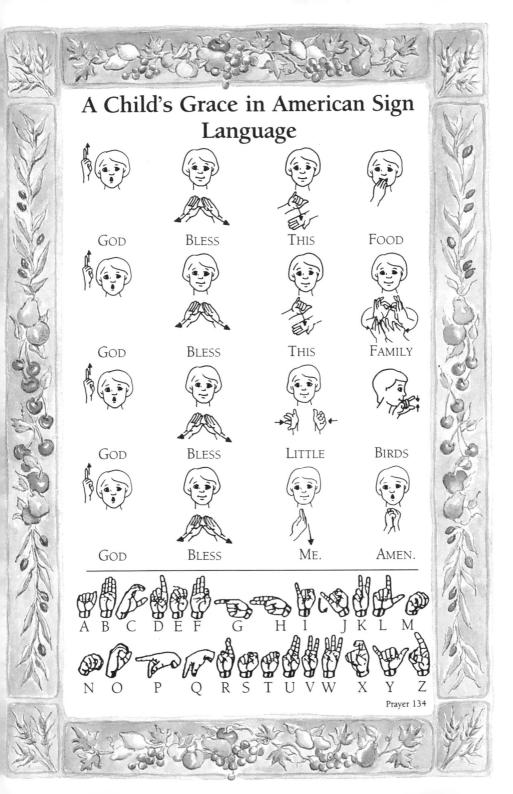

A Child's Grace in American Sign Language

GOD   BLESS   THIS   FOOD

GOD   BLESS   THIS   FAMILY

GOD   BLESS   LITTLE   BIRDS

GOD   BLESS   ME.   AMEN.

A B C D E F G H I J K L M

N O P Q R S T U V W X Y Z

Prayer 134

Bless This Food
in Nineteen Languages

Bless this food
English

Benedicite hunc cibum
Latin

Bendita sea esta comida
Spanish

Benis ce repas
French

Benedetto questo cibo
Italian

Segne diese speisen
German

Ευλογειτε Εκεινον Αρτον
Eulogayte Ekaynon Arton
Classical Greek

بارك هذا ألطعام
Barek natra aet'taam
Arabic

БЛАГОСЛОВИ ЭТУ ЕДУІ
Blagaslavee aetoo yedoo
Russian

בָּרְכוּ אֶת הָאוֹכֶל
Bareku et he'okel
Hebrew

टो स्यानेको आशिर्वादे दो
Ae kanae koo asheez doo
Hindi

Valsigna maten
Swedish

今日の食事に感謝いたします.
Kyoo no shoku ji ni kan
sha i ta shi ma su
Japanese

祝　福　食　物
Choo foo sheh oo
Chinese

Abencoe esta comida
Portuguese

Signe maden
Danish

Signe maten
Norwegian

Sivdnit biepmu
Samisk

Zaegen de maaltid
Dutch

Prayer 135

Index of First Lines

Notes on Prayers

Grateful acknowledgment is made to the authors and publishers for permission to use their copyrighted material. Every effort has been made to contact original sources. Omissions will be rectified in future editions.

Prayers to God in Heaven

1. William C. Segal is a philosopher, painter and writer who devotes himself to the study of man's place in the universe.
2. Abraham Isaac Kook (Rav Kook) 1865–1935. Mystic, philosopher, saint, Talmudic scholar. *Orot Hakodesh, The Lights of Holiness.* Paulist Press.
3. "Caedmon's Hymn." Caedmon (fl. 670). A lay brother at an English monastery who feared the custom of singing at meals until, in a dream, a voice instructed him to sing of the Creation. Transformed, he wrote inspired biblical verse, including this grace, which holds a distinctive place in English poetry as the earliest known text in English (composed in Northumbrian dialect).
4. The Bhagavad Gita is the "Song of the Lord (5th century B.C.)," a Sanskrit poem in the Mahabharata, one of the greatest religious classics of Hinduism. A Hindu concept is that food should not be eaten unless it be offered to God. It then becomes "prasad"—something to be eaten which was blessed by God.
5. Bhagavad Gita 3:13–14. The Gita illuminates Krishna's teachings, especially the grace of God. Sri Krishna (Sri is a holy title such as Lord) has been called the Christ of India owing to the remarkable parallels between the lives of Krishna and Jesus.
6. Traditional Jewish grace before meal. In Hebrew, this blessing is known as *ha-motsi* (bread). Reciting this benediction is in accordance with the rabbinic view that "it is forbidden for anyone to enjoy a good thing of this world without a blessing."
7. Jewish grace after meals (*Birkat ha-mazon*). A series of blessings and prayers recited after any meal which includes the eating of bread. The first blessing, traditionally ascribed to Moses, is of a universal character, praising God for sustaining all His creatures with food.
8. Burkina Faso, West Africa. Courtesy of the Embassy of Burkina Faso to the United States.
9. West African prayer. From *I Sing Your Praise All the Day Long: Young Africans at Prayer,* by Fritz Pawelzik. © 1967 by Friendship Press Inc. Used by permission.
10. *Armenian Prelacy Diary.* Permission of the Armenian Prelacy, Archbishop Mesrob Ashjian.
11. Prayer by St. Cyril of the Coptic Orthodox Church, Alexandria A.D. 412. The Christian church in Egypt traces its origins to St. Mark.
12. *The Thanksgiving Hymns.* The Dead Sea Scrolls (2nd century B.C.–1st century A.D.). A thanksgiving, composed by the author from the exact texts of couplets in a group of 66 fragments of eight devotional poems in biblical Hebrew that are characterized by their formulaic opening lines (I thank Thee, O Lord) and named the *Scroll of the Hodayat* (thanksgiving).
13. Numbers 6:24–26, Hebrew Bible. Taken from the New Revised Standard Version of the Bible, © 1989 by the Division of Christian Education of the National Council of Churches of Christ in the USA.
14. Terpander of Lesbos, c. 676 B.C. Greek poet and musician who invented the seven-string lyre, which revolutionized 7th-century music. Hymn to Zeus, the supreme deity in Greek mythology. *Wine in the Ancient World,* C. Seltman. RoutLedge & Kegan Paul. Used by permission.
15. Medieval Latin hymn, "Veni, Creator Spiritus," ascribed to Gregory the Great (7th century) or Hrabanus Maurus (9th century) translated by the English poet John Dryden (1631–1700). It has spawned many versions, the best known by Dryden.
16. The Book of Common Prayer, 18th century, Anglican and Episcopalian Churches. *Our Use of This World's Goods. Prayers for a New World* by John Wallace Suter, Macmillan Publishing Company, New York.

17. Christian prayer. This prayer employs a dramatic silent moment as a meaningful way to give thanks and reflect on life. Quakers use a wholly silent prayer. Prayer courtesy of Rev. John M. Allin, 23rd Presiding Bishop of the Episcopal Church USA.
18. The Lord's Prayer. Matthew 6:9–13. This essential Christian prayer is also found in Luke 11:2–4.
19. Graces for meals from Gelasianum Sacrementarium (6th century) confirm the early practice of table prayers among Christians. These graces are from the oldest extant altar book used in the Roman Catholic rite. Courtesy of Rev. Thomas A. Krosnicki, SVD, Divine World Missionaries.
20. Christian doxology. A hymn of praise to God. Doxa (Greek) means glory. Early Christian rites adopted from the synagogue the custom of ending each prayer with a doxa. *Gloria Patri et Spirtu Sancto* is known as the little doxology, the great doxology being *Gloria in Excelsis Deo.*
21. *B'kol Echad, In One Voice.* Ed. Cantor Jeffrey Shiovitz. United Synagogue of Jewish Conservatism. Used by permission.
22. From the *Liturgy of the Falasha of Abyssinia.* Falasha are Ethiopians of Jewish faith. Used by permission of Yale University Press. Introduction and sources translated by Wolf Leslau. Falasha Anthology © 1951.
23. Kankana-ey Tribe, Igorot Indians, Northern Luzon, the Philippines. All Igorot meals have religious undertones. Courtesy Bishop Narcisco V. Ticobay, Philippine Episcopal Church.
24. Author unknown.
25. *Prayers from an Island* (Hawaii), Richard Wong.
26. Universal Muslim prayer. Allah is the Arabic name for God. There are over eight hundred million followers of the Muslim faith worldwide.
27. Sufi blessing. Sufism, which dates from the seventh century, is the esoteric dimension of the Islamic faith, an inner spiritual path to a mystical union with God. Sufi ideas infuse Arab and Persian poetry.
28. Ancient Hawaiian harvest chant. This prayer thanks the gods for the harvest bounty and petitions for healing the land when it is ravaged by drought.
29. Tamil-speaking Hindu prayer. Tamil is the language of the Dravidian people of South India and Sri Lanka and is spoken by about 88 million people in India and 4 million in Sri Lanka.
30. A Gujarati-speaking Hindu prayer. Gujarati is an Indio-Iranian (Hindu) language descended from Sanskrit that is spoken by over 25 million people.
31. Prayer by Sri Ramana Maharshi. *Zohar, The Book of Enlightenment.* Translated by Daniel Chanan. Used by permission of Paulist Press © 1983.
32. George Herbert (1593–1633). The poet was a clergyman in the Church of England. Courtesy of Rev. John M. Allin, 23rd Presiding Bishop of the Episcopal Church USA.
33. William Shakespeare (1564–1616). *The Second Part of King Henry VI,* I. i. 19–20.
34. Text by John Milton, 1608–1674, English poet. Often sung as a hymn with music by J. S. Bach.
35. John Wesley (1703–1791). Founder of the Methodist Church and brother of Charles Wesley, he pioneered open-air preaching to common people in the fields.
36. Charles Wesley (1707–1788), the "sweet singer of Methodism" the most gifted and prolific of all English hymnwriters (7,270 compositions).
37. Author unknown. Christ's College, Cambridge, England. 1535.
38. The Book of Common Prayer, 16th century, used in both Anglican and Episcopalian churches.
39. Ancient Egyptian prayer to Hapi, the Nile God of nourishment, petitioning for the flood that enriches the fields.
40. African morning invocation. From *The Prayers of African Religion.* Used by permission of the Society for Promoting Christian Knowledge.
41. Prayer from China. Reprinted from *Mealtime Prayers* by Mildred Tengbom, © 1985 Augsburg Publishing House. Used by permission of Augsburg Fortress.
42. From Pakistan.
43. Alcuin of York, 735–804, was a medieval Christian scholar in the court of Charlemagne. A prolific liturgical writer, he invented a handwriting style called Caroline minus-

cule which used both small and capital letters, improving the readability of books through roman type.

44. See #21.

45. From the Mahabharata, the Sanskrit epic of India, the longest single poem in the world. It is the foremost source on classical Indian civilization and Hindu ideals. Composed between 200 B.C. and A.D. 200. Hymns to the Goddess (Sanskrit). Arthur & Ellen Avalon. Luzac & Co. London, 1913.

46. From the *Tantraasara*, an ancient Vedic Sanskrit text. In the Hindu faith the goddess Devi is creatrix and nourisher of the world analogous to the Christian notion of the "Mother of God." She bears the fruit of all knowledge. The goddess Annapurna provided food. (Rice = food in general)

47. The Gayatri Hymn. Rigveda III. 4.10. (c. 1500 B.C.). The holiest verse in the Rigveda, a hymn to the sun, the Supreme Being, usually personified as a goddess, wife of Brahma, the metaphorical mother of all. Said to have been inscribed on dry leaves, the Vedas are the most ancient ritual utterances of the early Aryans of India. From Sanskrit gai, to sing.

48. Deuteronomy 8:7–11, Hebrew Bible. NRSV © 1989 by the Division of Christian Education, National Council of Churches of Christ in the USA.

49. Dead Sea Scrolls (2nd century B.C.–1st century A.D.). Biblical Hebrew documents put in jars and hidden in caves by the Essenes of the Qumran community. Discovered in 1947, they hold an important place in the history of biblical writing and poetry for both the OT and NT. The Essenes were a pious sect who dressed in white and ate communal meals at which a priest said grace before eating. It was unlawful for anyone to taste the food before grace was said.

50. Ecclesiastes 11:1. Hebrew Bible.

51. Fourth-century prayer.

52. The Didache (Two Ways). A second-century manual of early Christian practice that included advice on aspects of church life, including food matters. Author unknown. Courtesy of Rev. Anne Sutherland Howard, Episcopal Church USA. The Didache (c. 150) is the oldest Christian literature outside of the New Testament.

53. Fred Pratt Green, 1903. Text copyright © 1970 by Hope Publishing Co., Carol Stream, IL. All rights reserved. Used by permission.

54. Author unknown. The tree imagery of this poem resembles a lovely passage in the Bhagavad Gita which describes a fig tree rooted in heaven with its branches earthward—clearly a food/grace God metaphor. See also #4.

55. Robert Burns (1759–96). *A Poet's Grace*. Scottish farmer, poet and songwriter.

56. *White Spirituals in the Southern Uplands: The Story of the Fasola Folk, Their Songs, Singings, and "Buckwheat Notes."* George Pullen Jackson. Dover Publications Inc. 1965.

57. A prayer of the Armenian Church (Lebanon), founded according to tradition by Apostles Thaddeus and Bartholomew. The Bible was translated into Armenian in the 5th century.

58. John 6:11, Christian Bible.

59. 1 Corinthians 10:31, Christian Bible.

60. Matthew 4:4, Christian Bible.

61. *Prayers & Graces of Thanksgiving*. P. S. McElroy (comp.). Peter Pauper Press. 1966. Used with permission.

62. Presbyterian prayer. Calvinist Protestant denomination of the national Church of Scotland.

63. Coptic Orthodox Liturgy, Egypt.

64. The 112 Upanishads are sacred scriptures of Hinduism, c. 900 B.C. They illuminate the doctrine of *brahman*, the ultimate reality of pure consciousness, and the identity of *brahman* with *atman*, the inner self of man. *The Principal Upanishad*. S. Radhakirshman, editor and trans., HarperCollins, 1989.

65. Prayer used in the Eucharist in India. Courtesy Longman House, England.

66. A praise song from the Balubas (Lubas), a Bantu-speaking people of Zaire. They were a cohesive tribe in the 17th century in the Congo.

67. *Prayer in the Religious Traditions of Africa*. Aylward Shorter. Oxford University Press: New York and Nairobi. 1975.

68. Prayer by Walter Rauschenbusch (1861–1918), American Baptist minister. Reprinted

from *Mealtime Prayers* by Mildred Tengbom, © 1985 Augsburg Publishing House. Used by permission of Augsburg Fortress.

69. Courtesy of Sister Judith Marie Saenz, Sisters of the Incarnate Word and Blessed Sacrament.

70. Henry Alford (1810–1871). English poet, hymnist and Biblical scholar chiefly noted for his monumental critical edition of the Greek New Testament.

Prayers in Thanks for the Bounty of the Earth

71. This prayer is said to the rhythm of "talking drums" every three weeks at a ceremony honoring the Ashanti ancestors, in Central Ghana. *Celebrating Nature*. Elizabeth Helfman, ed. 1969.

72. Pre-Hispanic Nahuatl blessing (13th century B.C.). The Nahuatl Indians considered food sacred and a gift from the Sky Father and Earth Mother, Quetzalcoatl. *Mexico's Feasts of Life*, 1989. Patricia Quintana, with Carol Haralson.

73. Nahuatl is the language of the ancient Aztec empire, still spoken today (Mexico). 16th-century manuscript in Nahuatl. Poesia Nahuatl, National Library of Mexico.

74. Mohandas Gandhi (1869–1948), Indian spiritual leader who asserted the unity of mankind under one God and preached Christian, Muslim and Hindi ethics.

75. Hindu prayer.

76. Rigoberta Menchú is a Mayan-Quiché woman from Guatemala who has become a voice of the poor and oppressed indigenous peoples of her country. She won the Nobel Peace Prize in 1992. *I, Rigoberta Menchú: An Indian Woman in Guatemala*. Verso, London.

77. Mother Teresa of Calcutta. In 1940, she founded the Catholic order Sisters and Brothers of Charity and has dedicated her life to the service of the poorest of the poor all over the world.

78. Excerpt from *The Spiral Dance* by Starhawk, a feminist author. Copyright © 1979 by Miriam Simos. Reprinted by permission of HarperCollins Publishers Inc.

79. A prayer of the Zinacanteán Indians. Courtesy of Fr. Joseph L Asturias O.P. Dominican Mission Foundation.

80. Reprinted from *Mealtime Prayers* by Mildred Tengbom, © 1985 Augsburg Publishing House. Used by permission of Augsburg Fortress.

81. Author unknown, c. 1400.

82. John Greenleaf Whittier (1807–1892). The American Quaker poet and bard of the common man composed over 100 hymns. *Everybody's Song Book*. George S. Dare, comp. 1938.

83. Iroquois. He'-no is the guardian of rain and thunder. Note that this prayer progresses from earth to the sky. Trans. by Ely S. Parker in 1851.

84. Ascribed to Muhammad (c. 570–632), founder of the Islamic faith. His revelations became the basis of the Koran, which is considered to be the direct word of God.

85. Psalm 104:13–15, Hebrew Bible.

86. Psalm 67, Hebrew Bible.

87. Adapted from the Gaelic.

88. Traditional hymn, England.

89. In this prayer an Indian addresses the deer he has killed. Out of respect for the life taken he begs forgiveness, and expresses pity. Permission from E. J. Brill Publishers. *Forgotten Gods: Primitive Mind From a Traveller's Point of View*. K. Herman Bouman, 1949.

90. This Osage Indian song is sung in celebration of the first corn of the season. It is sung by the mother as she runs to tell her children the exciting news of their new crop. *The Salishan Tribes of the Western Plateaus*, James A. Tiet, in *Forty-fifth Annual Report of the Bureau of American Ethnology* (1928–29). Washington, D.C. Courtesy of Smithsonian Institution Press, 1930.

91. Hildegard of Bingen, 1098–1179. German abbess and author of *Scivias*, an account of her twenty-six mystical visions. A prolific writer, she was one of the most original intellects of medieval Europe.

92. Author unknown.

93. Dante Alighieri, 1265–1321. *La Divina Commedia*, Canto XXVI. Used by permission of Christopher E. Knopf.

94. Permission of Father John Giuliani. The Benedictine Grange.

95. John Wesley (1703–1791). This blessing is often sung to the tune "Praise God from Whom All Blessings Flow." See #35.

96. Chief Dan George of the Tell-lall-wwatt Indians (Canada). Oscar nominee for *Little Big Man* and an eloquent spokesperson for the environment.

97. Buddha in *Itivuttaka, No. 26.* In Theravada Buddhism there is a strong emphasis on the practice of giving as an essential religious act and on generosity as one of the most admired spiritual goals. *The Itivuttaka: The Buddha's Sayings,* translated by John D. Ireland. Kandy, Sri Lanka: Buddhist Publications Society, 1991.

98. Grace of the Bodhisattva Buddhists (Seekers of Religious Enlightenment). Courtesy of Dr. Arthadarshan. The Office of the Western Buddhist Order. Norwich, U.K.

99. Chinook Psalter. Chinook are Native American Indians from Oregon.

100. Angelus Silesius, aka Johannes Scheffler (1624–1677), German mystic and poet. *The Cherubinic Wanderer* by Angelus Silesius, trans. by Willard R. Trask, © 1953 Pantheon Books. Copyright renewed. Used by permission of Pantheon Books, a division of Random House, Inc.

101. This prayer is known as the Five Reflections. Trans. by Eido Tai Shinano Roshe from traditional Rinzai Zen text. © 1982 by the Zen Studies Society Press. New York, New York. Used by their permission.

102. Millet prayer of the Ainos (Archipelago of Japan). Sir James George Frazer. *The New Golden Bough: A New Abridgment of the Classic Work.* Edited and with Notes and Forward, by Theodore H. Gaster, ed. © 1959 S. G. Phillips, Inc.

103. This is a harvest seed prayer of the Navajo and Blackfoot Indians. *The Writer & the Shaman.* Elémire Zolla.

104. Pre-Hispanic Nahuatl Blessing (13th c. B.C.). The Nahuatl Indians considered food sacred and a gift from the Sky Father and Earth Mother, Quetzalcoatl. *Mexico's Feasts of Life,* 1989. Patricia Quintana, with Carol Harolson.

105. *Prayer for the Sabbath. Book of Blessings: A Feminist-Jewish Reconstruction of Prayer.* Marcia Falk. Feminist American poet. Copyright © 1990 by Marcia Falk. Reprint by permission of HarperCollins Publishers Inc.

106. "Father's Clansman" is a respectful address to the sun. In this prayer a thanks-offering is being made to the sun. Translated from Crow by Robert Lowie, 1935. Used by permission of Irvington Press.

107. George Herbert (1593–1633).

108. Devotional Services, John Hunter. Permission of JM Dent Publishers.

109. Arapaho (North American Indian) chant. *Universal Folk Songster.* Florence Hudson Botsford, compiler.

110. Eskimo. *The World of the American Indian.* Copyright National Geographic Society. © 1974.

111. Marion Williams, American gospel singer. *The Gospel Sound.* Tony Heilbut, 1971.

112. A popular song among Christians against the belief that God is dead, which was gaining support in academia. Lyrics by Lawrence Reynolds. © 1969 by Tree Publishing Co., Inc. and Harlan Howard Songs. International Copyright Secured. All rights reserved.

113. An Igorot Indian harvest prayer from the highlands of Northern Luzon, the Philippines. A chicken is offered as a thanksgiving for a bountiful crop before being cooked for the family meal. Courtesy of Arvilla L. Cortez.

114. A corn ceremony chant, the Zuni Indians of New Mexico. Fifth Annual Report of the Bureau of American Ethnology (1883–84), Washingon, D.C., 1887. From *The Salishan Tribes of the Western Plateaus* by James A. Teit, in *Forty-fifth Annual Report of the Bureau of American Ethnology* (1928–29), Washington, D.C. Courtesy of Smithsonian Institution Press, 1930.

115. The Hako, a Pawnee Ceremony, from *Four Winds* by Gene Meany Hodge, courtesy of Sunstone Press, Santa Fe, New Mexico.

116. Ancient Hindu blessing.

117. Hindu poem. *Hindu Mythology: Vedic and Puranic.* Permission given by William Joseph Wilkins.

118. Abraham ibn Ezra, Spain (1092–1167). From his poem *God Everywhere*. He was a Judaic scholar and Spanish poet.

119. *The Book of Hours*. Congregation of Abraxas, a Unitarian Universalist Order for Liturgical and Spiritual Renewal. 1985.

120. John Lame Deer, Sioux Indian. From *Lame Deer, Seeker of Visions* by John Lame Deer and Richard Erdoes: Simon and Schuster, 1230 Avenue of the Americas, New York, New York 10020.

121. A Seneca poem of thanks. *Shaking the Pumpkin: Traditional Poetry of the Indians of North America*. Jerome Rothenberg. Reprint by permission of Sterling Lord Literistic, Inc. Copyright © 1972 by Jerome Rothenberg.

122. Christian prayer.

123. Monica Shannon. American author. *Words of Life*. Charles Langsworth Wallis. 1982.

124. Tecumseh (1768–1813). Chief of the Shawnee Indians.

125. Sacred Navajo food chant to attract the attention of the gods to make the fields fertile and the crops grow.

126. Prayer by Julian of Norwich (d.c. 1443). English religious writer, also known as Mother Juliana, who in 1373 had 16 mystical visions of Jesus, which she extoled in her Revelations of Divine Love. Reprinted from *Meditations with Julian of Norwich*, edited by Brandan Doyle, Copyright © 1983, Bear and Co. Inc., PO Box 2860, Santa Fe, NM 87504.

127. Arthur Guiterman, 1871–1943. *All About American Holidays*. Maymie Krythe.

128. Nancy Byrd Turner.

129. Excerpt from *Jambalaya* by Luisah Tesh, American writer. Copyright © 1985 by Luisah Tesh. Reprint by permission of HarperCollins Publishers Inc.

130. *Prayer Poems: An Anthology for Today*. Compiled by O. V. and Helen Armstrong. Copyright renewal 1970 by Helen Armstrong Straub. Used by permission of the publisher, Abingdon Press.

131. Rabbi Rami M. Shapiro.

132. Navaho Blessing of the Created World. Navaho people sing this prayer as a benediction to all forms of life in the world, declaring them beautiful. *The Indians' Book*. Natalie Curtis, ed. © 1968. Dover Publications. Used by permission.

133. Grace in sign language (ASL). Composed by the author. Grace and artwork copyrighted by Adrian Butash © 1993.

134. Child's grace in sign language (ASL). Composed by the author. Text of grace and artwork copyrighted by Adrian Butash © 1993.

135. BLESS THIS FOOD—a universal grace. The title of this book may be said as a grace, in any language, throughout the world.